# More Advance Praise for *Kill Class*

"Easily one of the most important books of our time." –CAConrad

"*Kill Class* is unsettling, arresting, essential. The poems insist we listen to war's distant cry, its close sigh, to the wreckage of language, to the questions buried and excavated, to worlds lost, to faces 'sent to sea,' to hearts incapable of translating other hearts. Nomi Stone is an invaluable voice."
—Nathalie Handal

"*Kill Class* is written with white-hot nerve, knife-edged precision, an anguished restraint, and a poet's implication of the untranslatable."
—Eleanor Wilner

"The sense of language as a portal permeates these poems written from the perspective of a speaker-anthropologist who struggles to understand the balance between recording the lives of others and engaging with those they seek to record. I'm interested in the many questions these poems excavate: of self-awareness, the practice of ethnography, the responsibilities of the modern poet-citizen, and the risks involved in grappling with the ever unwieldy, but perhaps still helplessly necessary, lyric 'I.'"
—Tarfia Faizullah

"Stone's stark and unflinching poems give a harrowing sense of cultural understanding made into a vehicle of state violence. The result is a truly arresting ethnography of American military culture, one that allows readers to circle at length through the cloverleaf interchanges where warfare nestles into the most mundane corners of everyday life, only to arrive at an exit where you would have expected least to find it: in an ethics of radical and transformative encounter, a way of coming undone in the company of others through the practice of sympathetic imagination."
—Anand Pandian

"In these poems, Stone dissects the violence and the vulnerability of being human with the stunning clarity and singular insight of her anthropologist's eye."
—Eliza Griswold

"I can't imagine reading a contemporary poetry book that I'll return to more."
—Rodney Jones

# KILL CLASS

POEMS

# NOMI STONE

TUPELO PRESS
*North Adams, Massachusetts*

*Library of Congress Cataloging-in-Publication Data available upon request.*
ISBN: 978-1-946482-19-8

*Cover and text designed and composed in Bembo by Dede Cummings.*
Cover and frontispiece photograph: Adam Fuss, *Love* (1993). Silver dye bleach print, 43 1/2 x 33 1/2 inches. Image made by placing two eviscerated rabbits on a photosensitized sheet of paper and exposing this to light. Copyright © Adam Fuss. Courtesy Cheim and Read, New York. Used with permission. All rights reserved.

First edition: February 2019.

TUPELO PRESS
P.O. BOX 1767, NORTH ADAMS, MASSACHUSETTS 01247
(413) 664–9611 / editor@tupelopress.org / www.tupelopress.org

Tupelo Press is an award-winning independent literary press that publishes fine fiction, nonfiction, and poetry in books that are a joy to hold as well as read. Tupelo Press is a registered 501(c)(3) nonprofit organization, and we rely on public support to carry out our mission of publishing extraordinary work that may be outside the realm of the large commercial publishers. Financial donations are welcome and are tax deductible.

Publication supported by the National Endowment for the Arts

ART WORKS.
arts.gov

: : :

# CONTENTS

## HUMAN TECHNOLOGY

Sunlit and dangerous, this country road.
We are follicle and meat and terror and

the machines leave their shells naked on the ground.
One soldier makes a museum in his basement.

Each mannequin in brass, incombustible coats:
I am walking between their blank faces,

their bullets traveling at the speed of sound. One soldier
who roasted a pig on his porch     barbecuing until sinews were tender

tells me he waited above the Euphrates and if they tried to pass
even after we told them not to, they deserved it: pop (deserve it); pop

(deserve it). Euphrates, your dark tunnel out is rippling around us.
In the war, a child approaches a tank as one soldier counts the child's

steps. In the town, I drink a bottle of wine with that soldier
among barber shops, boot repair shops. Is she my friend? I weep to her.

I've lost who I thought I loved and she says I did
this thing and to whom was that child beloved?

Find common ground, the soldiers say. Humanize
yourselves. Classify the norm of who you're talking to, try

to echo it. Do this for your country, says one soldier; we
are sharks wearing suits of skin. Zip up.

This spring, in the chilly, barely blooming city
Solmaz says enough of this emptied word "empathy."

Ask for more: for rage. For love. On the porch,
as the sun goes, the dark pools around us and one

soldier says it is nightfall. I am tired. I did not mean for it to go on
this long. That soldier across the table, we lock eyes.

He tells me: in the occupied land we are the arm, *they*
are the weapon. The weapon

in this case is a person. Choose a person
who knows who is bad. Make them

slice open the skin of their country: only they
can identify the enemy. Say yes or no: if a man squints while

under the date palm; if a woman does not swing her arms
while walking. Sir, my child was not with the enemy.

He was with me in this kitchen, making lebna at home.
The yogurt still is fresh on his wrist.

∴

                                                        Climb
                        in, climb out of the little black square —

        The village rises into form between the pines.
Cows and goats stand in the forest. Flimsy wood
and storage containers:   Muslim quarter   Christian
        quarter           Assemble /
disassemble. At a military technology fair in Orlando,
you can purchase a village in a box.
Just add people: live inside it for a time.


        At the beginning of the game, the soldiers are told half-
truths. They must stabilize who to trust and why before night
takes the stage.

        While playing market, Nafeesa and Hana cry out *lablābī
lablābī* to the soldiers. It's that roasted chickpea soup they sell
in paper cones in the Middle East. *Wīn a-lablābī, u ashgid?*" I ask.
"Where is the lablabi and how much?" They are so shocked
that they give me a Coke. We go in.

        POLICE STATION /                CRYING ROOM
        JAIL ROOM


        BROKEN-IN                       MOSQUE / SCHOOL ROOM
        INTERNET CAFÉ ROOM


        Omar tells me the soldiers don't know it yet, but all
the Iraqis in this village are in cahoots with the militia. The game says
figure out which bodies have turned the bright chill of gold.
In the classroom behind the imam's chair, a blackboard with drawings—
planes sizzling into the buildings.

        Omar shows me the knife, scimitar-curved, that hangs
on the wall at the police station. He takes down that knife, cradles it
like a guitar, plays a song.

## SOLDIERS PARACHUTING INTO THE WAR GAME

The fictional country stills
in the hour's resin. Men glide
through pinedark
into fields of cotton. Eyeless
seeds above: Is it, lord,
        snowing? They cross
into the mock village:
dome goat road row
Iraqi role-players whispering
in collapsible houses
made for daily wreckage.
Lights pulse, pixels
within them. In one room:
        a tiny fake coffin   no
isn't here a body   no, nowhere
here my   body.   Input: say
a kind word to the villager / output
villager soaked clean of prior forms
of place.   It is (subtract
this footprint) snowing.   Now
        fade.

## PINELAND, IN THE EMPIRE

Pineland has room for whatever the world does to itself. In the beginning, Pineland was somewhat like the Soviet Union. Now, Pineland is somewhat like the Middle East. Pins and pines are passing arms. Pins are dropping through the pines. A door in the woods opens. Each character lanterns awake—now cue the theater:

Laith.

Nafeesa.

Ahmed.

Hana.

Yusuf.

Omar.

Gypsy.

## THE ANTHROPOLOGIST

I bring my waterproof notebook, Arabic phrasebook, bug spray, a terror of snakes.
I drive the wrong way and the car is spat onto Sanitary Field Road, or onto the road
for Normandy or littler massacres. Or for the meat you eat after. Do I take it
with vinegar or sweet? Separate the shoulder from the rib. Spit me onto Pork
Chop Hill, Ham Road, Chicken Lane, Devil Way, and into the hold of these woods.
*So, what do you study? Is this part of a class for you?* Jeeps grow and grow under
the pines. It's true, they take me for BBQ after, ask me am I comfortable, do I want dessert
and what do I think I know about them and do I know any Americans who went
to war or don't I and if I don't who do I think I am, and do I agree that through my

stomach, they will get
my heart?

## WAKING

Bullseye, the sun takes
pavement and upturned
faces equally. Do not blame it
for knifing each next day open

across fruit stalls or asphalt.
Turquoise slivers between
blinds: light's clear ache
showers the sheets. You may

or may not find a lover, whose face
is here or here and here / and lit /
and dark.

## WAR CATALOGUES

Soldiers collect & number:
pigment, hair, jade,
roasted meat, timber,
cum. The enemy's
flute; the face

of an enemy
as he holds his young;
the enemy's face the moment
it's harmed. The woods

are a class in what
they can take. The country
is fat. We eat
from its side.

## MATRIX: WHICH IS WHICH

Pass the Taco Bell. Pass the wishing well: the door to Pineland, due South. Soldiers name me **Gypsy**. Gypsy, climb out of whatever cracked you. Can't you, Gypsy, let this road alone hold you? Dew in lace teeth, asphalt catches the sun. Feral green: synapse torches. Light lancing the village open.

:::

Don't talk to **Omar** who plays the bad guy. He belly laughs during the show. Omar is from the South / North / center of Iraq. Omar opens a barber stand under the trees between games, clowns around. Omar are you dead? Are you bad? Find out which is which. If Omar is from a village, it is the one where pear & date orchards were felled. If you hid there, between the bodies of birds you would feel cold spring light skinning your shins.

:::

**Yusuf** is the tribal leader of the village, comes from a long line & he holds much sway among the villagers. Attitude: cautious. He wants to help the Americans as he thinks this is the path to security & prosperity. Yusuf they want you to turn the people, open their locks.

:::

**Laith** snickers in the heat as upon his lean abdomen, spot-lit, they fix a wound. Quick, Laith you were first in your class, you wanted to study & understand the words in every Hollywood movie. You did it to help & you wanted to shine: you are of this country, carved from its side. The Human Terrain Team wants to write you down.

:::

**Ahmed** owns a shop in the village. His son was killed by an [errant] Predator strike. Death of his son has never negatively affected his view of Coalition Forces & he just wants to be left alone.

:::

Selling fake chickpea soup, swallowing air, **Nafeesa** in winter / Nafeesa in autumn. Wel-come to the slate gray sky propping up the game. Listen: something bad did happen to Nafeesa, or to someone else, or to all of them. Men in police uniforms take you to the Kill Yard. Take whomever worked w/ the Americans, no matter why & spinning nearly into N's spine in the aftershock of a spectacular wind, until my love——reboot.

:::

**Hana,** a mother, her eldest detained during night raid remains distraught b/c according to her her son was a good boy never did anything wrong why her son taken & where taken to

## MOTEL SIX AFTER THE WAR GAME

The field glows off and on
like fluorescent screens of televisions
in far-away apartments

After the games    I fold
into the smoky flowered coverlet
of the motel    floating across
the long black river of the highway

Today Omar ran in the woods
alongside the training boys    Yusuf
compared it to camping    Hana gossiped
about Laith    Laith pretended
to die    Ahmed cracked open
sardines to share in the grass
their spines melting immediately
to nothing    our mouths smeared
with salt    Omar pretended
to be a bad guy    Nafeesa    who they
all agreed at the Arby's afterwards
has a very bad story    fell inside
the game

Inside the flowered coverlet
before the day blinks black
I hold    the dream    of    a    you
in my center    I stop
the motel bed from going under
I keep the world above water
until I sleep

## BROKEN-IN INTERNET CAFÉ ROOM


A giant basket of fruit has poured open    plastic grapes
squeak to the floor

Yesterday the soldiers trashed the room and took the proprietor's
computer

Before the role-play, Laith speaks quietly   He tells me he translated for the Americans
during the war


When the play begins, his face

                          is sent to sea

## WAR GAME: PLUG AND PLAY

Wait. Begin Again.
Reverse loop. Enter the stage.
The war scenario has: [vegetable stalls], [roaming animals],
and [people] in it.    The people speak

the language of a country we are trying
to make into a kinder country. Some
of the people over there are good /
others evil / others circumstantially

bad / some only want
cash / some just want
their family to not die.
The game says figure

out which
are which.

## FORMER IRAQ WAR INTERPRETERS ROLE-PLAY EXECUTIONERS

Little war little

:::

tin murder, set them up,
knock them down. Unleaf

each life.
Willy

:::

holds out his iPhone. "Honey,
check it out      I played

killed."   In the video where he is fake-
executed, cloaked

:::

men brandish guns (It is the
Iraqi role-

players, L and O, crying out
in Arabic): *Tell the killer*

:::

*his end is nigh, spoke verily God
Almighty.*   Willy sits within

     his role his face
a moon his eyes upturned

     hands clasped   now shot
two times in the head falling

:::

     forward.   Wasn't that cool?
Are you writing this down?   Write it down     I

:::

write it, and:
     "During the war in 2003,

these fake
     executioners worked as interpreters (terps)

for the Americans—a killable
     choice."

:::

Some of them
     were dressed by the militias

in newspaper, scrawled with accusations, written
     in verse: *He who follows*

:::

     *them is one of them*
*Take not the Jews and Christians for your friends*

     *and protectors   they are but friends*

*and protectors to each*

:::

       *other   And amongst you*

:::

*who turns to them is of them.*   Brother, look into my eyes
       until the act is done.

## WAR GAME: AMERICA

*[Strip mall off the highway]*


With words
Ahmed explains
the holy books
say you can eat
someone alive
the sweet pound
deboned
a butter of what
was beautiful
Chew like a sheep

*[Under the pines]*

The Muslim Village has an hour break
Omar sets up his barber stand
he trims Yusuf's hair
he threads my eyebrows
Hana says do her upper lip
too    Hunger swells
the clouds    spidering
their shadows over
stripped mud fields
We joke sharply
in Arabic    The soldiers dreamed us up
They dreamed about Arabic
Say whatever you want
just say it in Arabic

## IRAQ, 2003

In their night gear, the Americans are
alien bugs. They open the shaken
house: a family offers them some juice.
Their terp's eyes blacken

       over the home. Keep

walking. Face forward.
Joe, a skinny soldier, Adam's
apple bobbing in throat
found his terp in the street turned

       to parts. Still,

Joe says: I do not trust our terps.
Say little, dear one.
Assume nothing. *Carry
your insides from market*

       *to market.*

# The Etymology of 'Alāsah, "Wartime Snitching"

*[Baghdad]*

The lexicons spoke
of its early
life: it meant to eat

especially wheat
three grains to
a husk. Such good

quality but so difficult
to cleanse. It is a black
grain, and you will

consume it but only when
desperate. It came to
mean embroidery,

a nervous raising
of needles into cheek
of cloth, metaphorically

the clicking of talking
like an itch, a twitch: bad
mouthing, getting

told on; also theft
of words; theft of
whomever you said

you were; no, theft
of who you truly
were; the limit of

cash for which you
give away my
coordinates.

## LOVE POEM

Undo the next time beauty
turns into tenderness turns
into a killing

# DRIVING OUT OF THE WOODS TO THE MOTEL

For your second job, you're a parking attendant or a poultry process worker: stun
and kill them, trim them and cut into portions, bone and weigh and grade them. You
are a hotel maid. If an American soldier stays in the room you clean, you will fold
his uniform as crisply as love, a message that you too call it a *liberation*. Your brother calls it
an *occupation*, tells you: Do not become American. Brother, the sanctions: 2 kilos sugar / 3
rice / 1 oil / 9 flour parsed into sections? Buy lipstick at the drug store. Watch Ramadan
soaps. Number your hungers. Braise the bird until it is gold with lemon. Unstring
your wish:

one bone liberation,
one bone occupation.

## POLICE STATION / JAIL ROOM

*[Come here first, they all say: it's the best theater.]*

Omar with the rumbly laugh, Omar who air-guitared the knife, waits at his desk.

Cue the soldiers. One approaches Omar: Sir,
we want to set up a tip-line. The people will be our
eyes.   How dare

you interrupt me, says Omar. *In the play you have to play hard
to get.*

Ahmed, thin as a wasp, role-playing O's guard, has the gun raised, barrel-
to-eye.   Please

lay it away, says the soldier. Who made you
king? asks O. Clicks the room, disengages
the lever.   Cue

the lights.   The lights are the signal
for Hana, splendid and peached-faced, the
bored half-laughing H in the prison, to crack

a scream; *inqathnī* rescue
me.   The wasp makes the scream
stop.

The soldiers do not know what to do with the not-
tamed   air, the H-
mute air.   O is playing

hard to get.   He says: It is normal. / It is natural. / You
can beat her with me.

A soldier shocks out
of his chair: Please can you not
engage in physical activity.
Another soldier shocks up:    We want to see
the person back there / we want to see her condition    O turns up
the juice: You can't let them in
your pants    No one made you
king here    the wasp clicks    the room clicks      send them through

                    the door / send them back /
in the door re-
load.      They smile at O with bright
cautious eyes    It is sure hot
today they say.    Sure, it is hot says O.    It's nothing like where we
came from in Ohio.

## CREATION MYTH (HOW ROLE-PLAYERS CAME TO SPEAK)

Soldiers build our legs and arms:
newly made, we clap the fire,
leg lift, leg lift, wake the ache
in the new hewn chest, circle
the pit, steep the tea, slice
the Spam into cheeks, break
the bread, then cry! Mouths
light open and shut,
open, then shut, around
their words, their words,
their words,
words, words . . .

## LIVING THE ROLE

The role-players play dominoes, trying to make the right numbers match.

Does anyone have a translation for any of this?  If your face is a mirror
(depending on whom you face), behind you is a splinter. This is one proverb.

Over there, if they asked you who you were, you would first have to know who they were.
Then, take your identification card out of your left pocket or out of your right pocket.

Of course we wish we could go home, Yusuf says. It would make me cry to taste an apple
from the North.

Living the role is like if you listen to a song and it was your song with your girl—
your brain tells you to stop   *you can't stop.*

## A Black Sun

"Do I know the Book," Ahmed asks "of the Sun?"
Drinking sugar tea, frying spam and eggs, men
play war, overthrow their own
governments. America enters by parachute:
soldiers dew the grass, dancing
as they fall, wrestling their jinn.

Jinn eat through the weak, blacken the sun:
one part of you goes, the other part, no: A halt, a freeze,
a place inside you you better not go. There's a difference
between an experience, friend, and an adventure. Diagram it:
A horror movie. A war game. Longing
that leaves teeth marks in. The jinn.

*Gypsy, count the hollows.* In each slot falls a sun.
"Fine okay, Ahmed, let's go to that movie." In the movie,
a girl drops down a well. Sit up, says Ahmed. Don't even blink
if you're afraid. For example if you're so, so tired
and you've stayed up for three days straight,
say: I am not tired. I am not tired.

## WAR GAME: AMERICA

*[Yusuf's apartment]*

*Pimps*, the Christians call the Muslims.
Or the reverse. I write the root
for the word,
singular then plural.

There is a door in every word;
behind it, someone grieving.

*[Under the pines]*

On the other side of the forest, men
scoop imagined ashes into a silver bowl.
A scenario hatched by the American military:
the Muslim village burns the Christian village.

Over the mock grave
they open the real earth
and plant fresh pinecones.
They cross themselves over
the needles / they sing Amazing Grace.

Wind spears over wild onion fields
and by the end,
pollen everywhere.
The carwashes in these parts
claim they get it off, completely.

### Do You Know How to Dance? Are You Married? What Are You Doing Here, and Do You Believe in the Prophet?

Outside, the girls are dancing:
     *yasār yemīn yasār yemīn.*
Watermelon and roasted corn
     and salt and salt and salt and salt.

Her purple earrings sparkle, Nafeesa's do,
     in the sun, there is sun,
I touch her arm. That is all,
     but / and / still, it is spring: light

catches in my chest. Whatever bad did
     happen, she is dancing too. We are
          none of us made of holes.

## THE NOTIONALLY DEAD

They call it the kill zone    I am going deeper in
We haven't slept    Pollen burns my nose

When shot in the head or torso at close range, die-in-place and no steak dinner

Dig 12 graves for those who did not cross
The light cools over the trees    They don't stop

my camera on upturning earth    bright orange clay    "Dude

you won't fit in there"    "Dude you're a big dude"
Write your eulogy, a pedagogical exercise to reinforce tactics

"So, where are you from?"    "Are you

the oldest?"    "Second oldest"    "What do you like to do for fun?"
"I like to run    I like Japanese food"    "How about

you?"    *Will you leave this life, too?*

Haven't eaten in hours, head a balloon on a string
rising into the arms of the trees    Soldiers are laid out shirtless

a little light from the fire    their nipples glow

*Isn't this strange to watch*, the anthropologist [I] asks
the Iraqis    Laith says come on

"Sweetheart nothing

about death is strange    I watched my cousin die    We couldn't
put him in the ground right away     We put him on ice"

## DRIVING OUT OF THE WOODS TO THE MOTEL

After the soldiers finish the game, neutralizing whomever they believe is a danger
to the free world, my friend & I drive out together, off the highway, past a sign
that says KIA. I say: "Killed-In-Action"? No. It is a dealership, bright cars in a
wide lot. As the city comes out of the gasoline haze: Days Inn, Walmart, Chick
Fil-A (the woods bluing to a point), we practice for his naturalization exam. Who
is the "Father of Our Country?" What are the principles of American democracy?
Renounce now, on oath, all prior loyalties. It is natural, friend, to want to live. How
neutral you wished to be, hired to bring your country to life. No preparing for how
the bomb packed with ball bearings & nails denatured the body. The acronym,
neutered, turns blank into a lot, but how

>                     we counted them,
>                     row by row.

## LOVE POEM

They straighten my hair and laugh when I make mistakes in Arabic. A wild gust out, but I forget the word. *Look at the perfumes shaking the leaves.* My best friends laugh: Write it down in your notebook! Come over every day! You are our talking doll!

While at Yusuf's house, I receive an email that changes my face. Y squeezes my shoulders hard. We take pistachios and olives to the rose garden.

Nafeesa, who is beautiful, tells me the word for goosebumps in Arabic.

Hana reads my future in the grounds of the gold-filigreed coffee cup. She says something astonishing will happen to me.

## KILL CLASS

The story says we are in the country of Pineland: grassy roads curving in, named
for longleaf pine, loblolly pine. Sassafras, blackgum, slashpine,
clethra sharp as pepper, shallowing
the land's breath.

The story says I join the guerillas.
The story says I carry this tent in.

Three cages at the wood-line:
the goat, the chickens,
a solitary white rabbit.

> Commander: *You are Gypsy, from Taylor-town, the widow of Joker,*
> *one of the fallen guerillas.*

They make me a fighter.
One woman among 40 guerillas
and the 12 American soldiers
secretly training them to overthrow
their country's government.

Joker fell heroically, and our child—there was a child—they made me eat his ashes.
I am supposed to arrive at the guerilla camp full
of fury, and if possible, to cry.

> Commander: *Do you take hot sauce on those ashes?*

It's May. Heat saps the water out of the body
as pines swoon in and out
and out. They have put aside the rabbit for me.

> Commander: *Gypsy, this is yours. Feed it. For now, feed it.*

The trainees help me set up my tent.
They give me noodles to eat.

> Trainee: *Sweetheart, do you know you get fired if you break role?*
> *We need this work. We hold onto it like a tick. If you break*
> *role you fail this course. Stay right here together in this wood.*

I break my camping fork.
Gentle-faced Whisker gives me another.

> *What did you do    before the war?*

No one told me what I was supposed to have done
before. I decide on the truth,
so I can better retain it: I was a student, I tell them,
writing about war. The men come to fetch me.
It is time to tell my story:

standing in the wood, something in me,
delicate and moving and hot. I
have spent my time considering the role-
players crying on a loop. It is a play.
*If possible, cry.*

> Commander: *Gypsy, two plus two does not equal five. Certain stories*
> *make no sense.*

Sense    is an edge, see
        if you dare    look
        over into the white
        falling    We are in
        a role-play
        *but if you feel it in there, you feel it.* What is it
        you think I am lying
        about, Commander?

His eyes flash:    *So you are an anthropologist?*

I say: I am here writing about the Iraqi diasporic population—
they received asylum to Pineland after 1991.

Are they Sunni or Shia?

I say, both.

Do you see
how easy it is to catch you?

Listen, I know the Iraqis in Pineland are mostly Shia
but many intermarried before they came.

Julie, two
plus two does not equal five    Do you know
what we do to traitors?

My name isn't Julie, I tell them.
My name is Gypsy.

      Time's come: we're going on a six-hour mission.
*Carry your water on your back.*

I approach the Commander / I say I'm sorry
to break role for a moment. I'm a student from New York,
and I appreciate the chance to play,
but I am not the most rugged person in the world,
and I am the only woman here,
and I would like to have a bit of control
over what I do and don't do.

      Commander: Young lady, you have started out on the wrong foot.
Don't tell me who you're not.

Trainees: Suit up, Gypsy. Spray this on,
it is 100% DEET.

We go. I can't
keep up with the group.   Gypsy you stay
right behind me      Everything
will be all right.   I try to make small
talk because other talk brings me out

/ you have to stay in.

Drink your water / Follow
me / Dissolve
your super hydration tablet
Drink your water / Push on
Tell your body   you are fine
*You are fine.*

The wood is long and tall: it's shot with light.
Light makes little lances through the leaves.

Whisker and Commander say Gypsy,
we need to have a talk. You come here
with this sob story. No one knows really, and none of it
matches up.   Two plus two does not equal five.
A reporter named Julie went missing a few days ago.
Rumor has it that she joined up with a guerilla group
in order to get a story. We're pretty sure you're Julie.
Or, you're with the government
police.      No,

I say.   No.   I am Gypsy.   My husband was
Joker. I am from Taylor-town.

Gypsy, you know
what we do to traitors.
Give me your notebook.
I am not asking.

They bring me to the tree-line for kill class.
Gypsy this rabbit is yours. We have all been kind
enough to share our food and water out here.
We all have to help out so we can eat.

There is a pit for the un-useable
            portions of the entrails.    Secure the goat, slit its neck over
            the pit, and proceed with the chickens.

This one is yours.
Use this stick. One time over
the head should be enough.

*Make the spy cry.    Make the spy cry.*
*The pines simmer and contract.*

You have to, Gypsy, they say.
You can do it. Commander tries to give me
a fist bump to say We
are in this together. We are not in this together.

They cannot make me lift
my fist. Gypsy
how can we trust you? If you can't kill
an animal, how
can you be a fighter?

The pines.

I'm sorry. I will clean it after if you want.

Commander is shaking. He returns
the rabbit to the cage.

They bring me over     the chickens warm and still
The flesh under
their feathers
the organs
pulled out / the pearled
interiors.     This is meat now. I turn them
into something

we eat. I think I am done,
but Whisker says almost gently
*Gypsy you need to kill the rabbit. Unfortunately*
*you do not have a choice.*

I have a choice.     Let me be perfectly clear,
I say. It is not happening.

The men make a circle
The pines make a circle
You need to hold
the legs.     They are tying together
the legs     the animal
screaming     They raise
the stick     The legs are in
my arms     The legs are in my arms

⋮ ⋮

## CRYING ROOM

The tank accidentally did it.
To start the story again, press play.
*Crying Room* is a booklet that tells how
a body is undone by plot.
In order to succeed in the scenario,
the soldiers must also acquire information.

Wailing is a noise between them and information,
and consolation is impossible when you play
someone who is home    and you can't cry
for home, except sometimes, when undone
quite accidentally,
in between laughing. The scenario

needs verisimilitude. The writers of the scenario
care about affect as much as tactic.
If you cry for real or accidentally, you get a military coin.
Play it like you lived it.
(You lived it.) You have information.
Between you and information is the undone room.

## COUNT YOUR KILLS

We disassemble each other:
we make each other disappear.
In the room lit like an oven
we kill what we hold
in our arms, gentle body
of sand and wind.

## LOST OBJECT

*[Former 2003 Iraq War interpreters, current Role-Players]*

To taste it would make me
North        Where is that acre    of sweet
marrow    Bone-meadows
snowier each day    green
curls into    knife

Iraq is ripe
we carry it through
the simulacra of woods
At this time of year
you could wash orchards in the icecreek
till your *wrist* aches *cold and absolutely the mouth*

*of knowledge*      if your neighbor
learns about what you're doing
with the Americans—careful now,
this is war—he might eat you    you
are the last fruit left on this street.

## MASS CASUALTY EVENT

Watching from inside
the game, billowing gasses
for camouflage, clouds
of green, luminous clouds
of yellow, the flushed face
of the Major's child, our faces,
white-gold torches in the meadow.

I am in war. No,
I am in a game
of war. No, I am in a painting.

## ON THE 4TH OF JULY IN THE EMPIRE

The soldiers, as a joke,
bring a pig on the plane,
to tandem-jump
with one of the dudes.
Bucking, manpig
twists through air

'til pig won't / man can't.
Skin, socket, a tremble of teat.
They tell me this in a bar
right outside of these woods
where old boys act-out
a rape to teach war's

do's and don'ts, slapping
their hands together —
Are you in on this joke?
*Do you love your country,
Gypsy?* Drink up before
the animal lands.

## THE PINES MAKE A CIRCLE

*They load their guns with blanks.*
*There's nothing here to fear.*


You're driving weird, Gypsy: you're weaving.


*Nothing here to fear*
*but the mind fills in the gaps.*


Whichever way you turn, soldiers
dream-walk in and out of the poem. The dark
is sweet: a nerve inside a tooth.


*If midnight comes, tell it*
*what you saw: hooded, quartered*


face-down in gravel. Break
the ice with the bad guy. Then when


*it's time, a tooth for a tooth.*

## SHOCK: WAR GAME

"The wound . . . occurred suddenly, invisibly; it
came out of nowhere."    Rooms in the woods

help you prepare to hold it together for whatever
comes from off-center.

Mewling goats, villagers crying in their language for
water. The chest-opening

call to pray de-
leafs, snapping

you when missiles
follow. If your body

is an animal, talk to it
your trembling away.

## THE HUNTER DRESSES AS HIS PREY

Rocking, the body is hide,
palmed horn, jaw &
gum, thrashed-up antler,
till under the hat: a human
mouth half-
breathes in the firs. Face
to face, both not &  yes,
both dead & loved, am I
your calf / I am your calf.

# DRIVING OUT OF THE WOODS TO THE MOTEL

*[Character 1, Game 2, puts the keys in the ignition]*

Get gas. Get a Coke. Drive past American houses, shut in a chokeweed of chickens and trash. To the highway and turn the radio up. Make a to-do list. Tuition, groceries, pin number, food stamps, and your cousins wait on Skype. You could get another job. You could make your wife proud. But the Walmart application has 70 questions. Does Walmart think it is the White House itself? For example, the unhappy customer comes up to you and says: Walmart has bad service. Do you: a) Give the customer a form to lodge a complaint? b) Tell the customer that Walmart is understaffed today and apologize? c) Apologize and say Walmart is doing its best? Save money, live better. Be a checker at the grocery. Go to the center of the weather, be a good father, be a good daughter, honor your mother, call her on Skype. You are Moe. You are Joe. You are Raki, for short. You were the best damn interpreter the soldiers ever saw. They trusted no one, but they trusted you. Live with honor, live in God's hands. But why did they hire the other guy? Why did your child almost die but

not die when the bomb
sheared this sky upon them?

## MOSQUE / SCHOOL ROOM

Find all the Iraqis in this village: they're in cahoots with the militia.
In the imam's classroom, a blackboard with drawings of planes sizzling into
the free world.

These are the codes, clues, but I can follow nothing. It is night. Outside
the quadrant, the black roads circle

back into the base, whichever one you take. I have not eaten in a long time, and one
soldier hands me a clementine, the juice dribbles over my notes. I hear four

rooms at once. To my left, grapes strewn in the café, his face at sea. To my right, they live it
quite accidentally. Across the hall, the wasp clicks in the H-mute air. Square

of murmurs / square of cries. Square of falling and rising, falling then rising. Climb
in / climb out of the little black square no matter what you encountered there. The soldiers

try to befriend the imam and crack the code. Afterwards, the imam
chides them: You should have shaken my hand. Their Commander reminds them

to use rapport to get to the main point. Drink tea with them for an hour
at the very end, maybe you will get what you need.

I am learning how to be an anthropologist. Anthropologists are furious and want
culture back. Every day in this wood, I drink tea, fragrant and black / and wait very slowly

for them to open, and for me to open; it is a green ache and it is nothing if not need.

## WOUND KIT

*[Simulaids Deluxe Casualty Simulation Kit: $760.00]*

Stick-on Wounds: Eyeball (900), Foreign body protrusion (901), Eviscerated intestines (902), Large laceration, 5 cm (903), Medium laceration, 3 cm (904), Small laceration, 1 cm (905), Compound fractured tibia (906), Small sepsis wound (909), Large sepsis wound (910)...

They'll paint on the guts. Laith is rib-lean and theatrical.
    Choose him.

A First Class Private, his braces glinting, kids: "Die, & I
    will dig you a shallow grave."

Position Laith in the grass where he falls. Fiddle with his cell phone.
    It is hot. It is pre-set.

His fake wife Nafeesa makes a puking face. Around the field,
    the trees sweat.

They chose him because he knows about real war. In Iraq, leave
    in an hour or be killed. Roulette.

"What do you take with you? Your laptop? Your mother?"
    Then, re-set.

Training soldiers arrive around Laith's body. Villagers flick droplets
    from their water bottles across Laith's face.

Nafeesa asks a soldier: "Ha yemūt?" [*Will he die?*].
    The soldier can't understand / thrusts paper and pencil at her.

If she writes it down he can look it up.
    Nafeesa says: "Turīd arsimh?" [*You want me to draw
it?*].

## What Is Growing in These Woods

Green in here, gleaming
like being inside a fable
with stalls of fruit you can't eat.
To go home, leave crumbs.
When the wood circles you
back here instead, let the lost
and the impossible ripen
in you, ripen and go.

## THE DOOR

Goats mewling
in the Muslim village.
Leafy footpath
into the bodiless acre
of graves. Pass.

Animals:
goats
chickens (a fury, a pack)
one pig (Salma)

     Instructors measure our fervor.
     *Your machine must cover*
     *the kill zone*   *100%*   Notate this fever   Carry

     the lure of the apple.
     Where are you Salma? Little ache
     of sky. Killing
     Field inside, branches latched. Arbor, what is beyond
     this wood?

Anthropologists practice at the circling
pinwheels of faces; those at war are matchless.

     Laith has skulls and flags flesh graven.  In the war, L
     worked with the Americans   So did O / so did H / so did
     _____.

        We split and cast away
       salt seeds over the needles.
       Get more at the gas station a mile outside. Outside,
       there are bursting cotton bolls,

molecule to sepal
sepal to stalk
blowing their little snow over
the red clay. Out there,
a gas station    breathing roads

Even you, dear you; you
have been waiting a long time
for me, haven't you?
Take this road into the body / return it
as a love
letter. Body
a simmering lake
of code, nutrient,
wishing. In Arabic,
there is a word that means the cleaving
from dormancy or sorrow
into first joy.
Or, the arriving
mouth of the messenger.
It is right on the other side of this wood.

# IRAQ, 2003

Below the storm, blind bodies
inside a yellow cloud.
But the eyes of the bombs saw
inside the cloud
into the dark
intentions of the bodies.

If you slit a fish longitudinally
and place its seamed belly
across a plate,
any radioactive tissue
will expose on film:
cells forgetting

themselves, blinking
gold gold gold.
Like the tainted thistle
diving its roots 20 feet down
sucking strontium-90 and cesium:
in it came, through the hollow
throat of the plant:

in came the soil's
dark drink.
How they snipped off its
seeding head.
These are those
people / these are
those people.

## CREATION MYTH (SOLDIERS BEGIN AGAIN)

When dead, lie shirtless
in a clearing / whisper
your eulogy to your partner
so just as the sun
comes up, the blinking
blue God-Gun reboots.

## AFTER THE WAR GAME

*[Billy's House, the Soldiers Tell Me What They Think of Me]*

I.

Outside the game there are miles
of barber shops / boot repair
shops and today Billy
is cooking chili. Come on over
and join your buddies.
Commander came special for you.

In the back room men banter hard
smoke and laugh hard *Come*
*on in* they guffaw
calling me the Marxist-Muslim *ha*.
I say (half girlishly because

that's the way in) I want
to hear your version of what
happened there. Can I take
notes? Billy looks pissy /
Commander says Oh yeah ha
that notebook of yours
no way    this is old boys talk

and we're recording you
then one of them laughing
pulls a 45 out of the drawer
*This is loaded*    They look at me.
We inside the rough ongoing joke
now wink.

II.

"They had no use for you, kid,"
says Billy, "they want you
dead. You're
all questions; you're no
answers. The word was

out. They knew
the part
of you

you keep hidden.
Break this one
until she hardens.
You were
the fly in the punchbowl.
They want you
shot and we are more
than family."

Billy, you
and I sit
at this checked tablecloth,
drinking black coffee
eating biscuits and gravy
while you show me

old photos of your dad
in his brass,
while you ask your wife

if she wants a bowl.
War somewhere,
the year 2014.

August light falls mellow
across the pot of stew,
and the mewling kitten and the acres
of longleaf pine.

## PLUG IN THE ROLE AND PLAY

*Plug in:* Kill. *Play:* King. Play beating
heart in my shoulder, painted
wounds circled by bees.

You asked the part
of me I kept hidden. It was every
softness I didn't give them,

the life awake,
whole,
trembling.

## THE SOLDIER TAKES THE ANTHROPOLOGIST TO THE SHOOTING RANGE

After shooting, we go to the buffet, and there is so much meat: chicken and fat and cuts of hog, then banana pudding with crumbled cookies. We eat so much it is awful, almost.

What do I want with this place?
I've got a candle in me. It won't quit.

Later we walk through his tomatoes, lush and stemmy. There's one fruit, green.
I came again and why? To be next to it, whatever "it" is and not die? *You look for the dark,* Billy says, *in things.*

The wick is lit
like a gun.

The targets, once birds: changed into silhouettes with red kill-spots, heart-shots. Billy knows what it (he) does and did / the hole in the throat / the eyes so surprised.

*If you hold it wrong,*
*it will bite your thumb.*

He presses my back. It goes when I press.  I jump when it goes. The round so splits her: nerves / root / where to take cover, in this field of copper teeth?

*Don't shoot so high.*
*You're aiming at God.*

Then, I went in. Did I know what I did? It rang with a ping. Bullseye, red as a torch.
He threw up his arms.  I was I.  It was done.

## THE CAMERA BURNED A HOLE

*[The Anthropologist Follows Baghdad's Lost Books and Refugees]*

On the day we fell through
the vortex, a friend forecast our futures
from traces of coffee
in lacquered cups:
three journeys and twin daughters.
When we fell, we fell past
inseparable rivers and *dusk in trees,*
*water in jars / spilling rain bells.* Falling,
we passed boats sluicing
over drained marshes,
orchards which re-sprout
just as they're leveled.

And why did you work with the Americans?

"I did it to feed my family." "I drove a truck for an Iraqi company that supplied the
US military." "I did not know who I was working for exactly." "Who doesn't love
a good bootleg Hollywood movie?" Inside our dream of country, a tiny bird sings
harshly with oracle.

Can you tell me about *The Drawing of Lots* by Ibn al-Mutāhil?

Supple, the air, the morning
they drew lots. An Ambush
scheduled for that day.
We stood in the giant field
of wild onion
in the exact middle
of those curls
of grass-scent and weeping.
Everyone pantomiming

morning.

Al-Mutāhil disorients us before we are given
our lot. It's a Mass Casualty Event.
We will lose our limbs.
*This machine covers 100% of the Kill Zone.*

You just bought a ticket to the show.

What did you do before the war?

Libraries fattening
like roses, al-Mutanabbi Street
had not yet been fed to the sky. "Not one

I loved had yet been lost." We trusted

our friend, who walked between
villages and towns repairing every
broken thing:

crushed clasp, fragmenting

wedding song. "Those days, the President cut
the dates and orchards so no one could hide
inside them." *When they smile, your eyes,*

*the vines put forth their leaves.* Why
do you think this has anything to do with you?

Who were you, after *The Varieties of Creeping Things*, by Ibn al-Batrīq?

That which crept
could not always be named.

There was a catalogue: the squirming and the beetling,
the under-strata in the mulch, the simmering

among the needles of the pines, the metallic-smudged
handprint on the door, the traitor wrapped in sacred verses,

the white worm of pain
inside your skin, the almost-lit

match in your chest,
in that moment you did not speak.

Your mother, who is the most tender
and most persevering person you know
cannot put a wall between you and the creeping things.

Our author wants you to know:
you are on your own.

Do you expect to one day return?

"I went back to sell my land."
[iPhone photo: Date Palm.]
"I felt nothing."

"Grab your camera! Get ready
to film this!" says the soldier, observing the War Game.

"Two of them are still moving around. Haven't they bled out by now?"
In the truck, each laughs off her death as the game ends.

:::

    :::

        :::

But the camera burned
the hole. We fell through.

Anthropologist, why are you in this story?

Forest: War blinks
through each
of my friend's losses:

      leg,
      house,
      son.

Press Record: A spartan room, flowered mattress pad, droning TV and fan; rain spots,
mold spots. Their living son does not turn from the TV.

"I did it to feed my family. I did not know who I
was working for exactly. They found us. It
happened in the morning." Batteries stutter:
the recorder beeps.

"Son, hurry, find her
a battery." Press: I will never understand
and how dare I come here. Lord, I

came here. I knew not loss. These woods are lit by you, and you.

And who are you now, on the other side, *Coming on Objects Unexpectedly*
*(verse)* by unknown?

Out of the sonorous dark came the objects: the bells
beneath the river; the bridge (it is your childhood bridge):

the men and women and children crossing
the bridge on that holy day—

someone yelled: "It is a trap"
and do you know, they jumped that moment

out of their deaths,
the river took them.

From the darkness came the lightdrunk hole
out of the whitehot nerve; came keepers

from the Yusifiyya farm, their bees fanning
the air. Amber-yellow, almost bitter under the sweet,

it can cure your sore throat:
if you eat the eggs of the bees right from the comb

(he explains; have I translated this correctly?)
you will have a very strong heart.

:::

## NOTES

*Kill Class* is based on two years (2011–2013) of ethnographic fieldwork, observing predeployment exercises in mock Middle Eastern villages at four military bases across the United States. The setting of these poems is the Middle East-inflected, US military-created fictional country of Pineland, in the woods of the American South, where people of Middle Eastern background are hired to theatricalize war for the training soldiers, repetitively pretending to bargain and mourn and die. The anthropologist, the speaker in the poems, alternately observed and participated in the war games, and was a student of the culture that these games had put to their own uses. While the poems are based on extensive interviewing of military personnel and role-players, all characters depicted herein are fictionalized and hybridized, and all exercises and incidents described are composite and altered versions of actual war games.

The Arabic in this book mainly follows the transliteration style from *International Journal of Middle-Eastern Studies* (IJMES), with modifications for Iraqi dialect.

### "HUMAN TECHNOLOGY"
There are several direct quotes here. A military psychologist instructed training soldiers to: "Find common ground. Humanize yourselves. Classify the norm of who you're talking to. Try to echo it." In an interview about empathy, a soldier replied: "We are sharks wearing suits of skin." Thank you to Solmaz Sharif for her conversations and writing about empathy. This poem is for her.

### "MATRIX: WHICH IS WHICH"
Half of the characters in this poem (Yusuf, Ahmed, Hana) are drawn from military character sketches and hybridized.

### "War Game: Plug and Play"

The title draws on a common phrase in the military war game lexicon: "plug and play," wherein you substitute different entities (characters, events, etc.) into a scenario and play out the outcomes.

### "Former Iraq War Interpreters Role-Play Executioners"

The line "Tell the killer his end is nigh spoke verily God Almighty" is likely a weak/ unverified *hadith* (see www.saaid.net); I am uncertain of its exact origin. I did not find this exact *hadith* among al-Bukhārī's Saḥīḥ, though the following hadith is there: "Wherever you find them, kill them, for there will be a reward for their killers on the Day of Resurrection" (Saḥīḥ al-Bukhārī, Volume 6, Book 61, Number 577). The quotation "He who follows them is one of them. Take not the Jews and Christians for your friends and protectors: they are but friends and protectors to each other. And amongst you who turns to them is of them" is oral partial re-narrating of Al-Ma'ida (5, 51) in the Qu'ran.

### "Living the Role"

The phrase "if your face is a mirror, behind you is a splinter" is a play off the Iraqi proverb "Your face is a mirror and the back of your head, a splinter" [*bil-wajh mirīyah u bil-gūfa silāya*]. The subsequent three lines are quotations or near-quotations from role-players.

### "A Black Sun"

This poem references the "Book of the Sun," a thirteenth-century Gnostic text written by Ahmed al-Buni, which is composed of magical squares which are portals to the jinn, those invisible beings made of smokeless fire who possess humans. The Encyclopaedia of Islam describes the volume as "materials for the magical use of numbers and letter-squares, single Kur'an-verses, the names of God and the mother of Musa, indications for the production of amulets, for the magical use of scripts" ("al-Būnī," in Encyclopaedia of Islam, Second Edition, edited by P. Bearman, Th. Bianquis, C. E. Bosworth, E. van Donzel, W. P. Heinrichs. http://dx.doi.org/10.1163/1573-3912_islam_SIM_8428).

Formerly banned in Iraq under Saddam Hussein, the book bore a nearly flammable quality for Ahmed.

### "The Notionally Dead"

Quotations are from soldiers overheard during the exercise. The quotation from "Laith" occurred during a related but not identical exercise, which represented death.

### "Lost Object"

The phrases "wrist aches cold" and "absolutely the mouth of knowledge" are plays on language in Elizabeth Bishop's "At the Fishhouses."

### "Shock: War Game"

"The wound . . . occurred suddenly, invisibly; it came out of nowhere" is from Wolfgang Schivelbusch's *The Railway Journey: The Industrialization of Time and Space in the Nineteenth Century* (University of California Press, 1986).

### "The Hunter Dresses As His Prey"

This poem is inspired by Nils Bubandt and Rane Willerslev's "The Dark Side of Empathy: Mimesis, Deception, and the Magic of Alterity," in *Comparative Studies in Society and History*, Volume 57, Issue 1, January 2015.

### "Wound Kit"

The Simulaids Deluxe Casualty Simulation Kit epigraph is taken from the Simulaids website. In this poem there are several near-quotations from soldiers and role-players.

### "The Door"

"Your machine must cover the kill zone 100%" is quoted from a soldier supervising training exercises.

### "Iraq, 2003"

This draws from descriptions in Joseph Masco's *Nuclear Borderlands* (Princeton University Press, 2006).

### "After the War Game"

The poem draws on quotations and/or near-quotations from soldiers.

### "The Camera Burned a Hole"

Here there are several lines from the Iraqi poet Badr Shakr al-Sayyab (from Lena Jayyusi's translations in the 1987 anthology *Modern Arabic Poetry*, but with the article "the" omitted in the two second clauses): "dusk in the trees, water in jars / spilling rain bells" and "When they smile, your eyes, the vines put forth their leaves." The poem was inspired by a call for submissions by the Asian American Writer's Workshop, "Calling All Literary Baghdads," which invited writers to use the titles of books from Ibn al-Nadim's 7,000-book catalogue Kitāb al-Fihrist to inspire new poems; the actual books were lost during the sacking by the Mongols in 1258. The titles I used in the poem are *The Drawing of Lots* by Ibn al-Mutahil; *The Varieties of Creeping Things* by Ibn al-Batriq; and *Coming on Objects Unexpectedly* by an unknown author. There are also several quotations and near-quotations from US soldiers and Iraqi role-players in the poem.

: : :

## ACKNOWLEDGMENTS

Poems from this book have appeared in the journals *Anthropoid, Bear Review, Blackbird, cellpoems, diode poetry journal, Drunken Boat, Guernica, Hermeneutic Chaos, Memorious, Painted Bride Quarterly, Plume, Poetry Northwest, Post Road, Sixth Finch, and South Writ Large.*

Thank you first to the extraordinary editorial team at Tupelo—Jim Schley, Jeffrey Levine, Kristina Marie Darling, Cassandra Cleghorn, Dede Cummings, Samantha Kolber and Marie Gauthier—for believing in *Kill Class* and shepherding it into the world.

My enormous gratitude to those who have been my essential, exacting, and loving readers of this manuscript from beginning to end (and are so dear to me otherwise): Eleanor Wilner, Lisa Hiton, Holly Shaffer, Gretchen Marquette, Raena Shirali, Rebecca Gayle Howell, Kate Murr, Jennifer Funk, Cleopatra Mathis, Jorie Graham, Rodney Jones, Sameen Gauhar, Rachel Richardson, Allison Titus, Bridget Purcell, Rebecca Linder, Philip Metres, Emilia Phillips, Sean Singer, Joseph Capista, Bernadette Perez, Jennifer Rumbach, Nadia Jamil, Rose Skelton, Elaine Stone, Warren Stone, Lia Stone, and Zach Stone.

Thank you to other crucial readers of my poems along the way, in particular my extraordinary MFA advisors at Warren Wilson: Monica Youn, Roger Reeves, Gabrielle Calvocoressi, and Alan Williamson. Tremendous thanks also to Ellen Bryant Voigt and Deb Alberry and my Wally family—every last one of you—for changing my life.

Thank you to my two writing groups: Raena Shirali, Shevaun Brannigan, Daniel Brian Jones, Alan Beyersdorf, Irene Mathieu, Tim Lynch, (and also Julia Kolchinsky-Dasbach), my core and strength in Philadelphia; and Sara Eliza Johnson, Paige Lewis, and Sumita Chakraborty in the beautiful ether. And other crucial readers and poetry interlocutors these many years: Sarah Green, Daniel Jenkins, Luke Hankins, Natalie Diaz, Esme Franklin, Tiana Nobile, Jehanne Dubrow, Mellie Ivy. And my gratitude to other still unmentioned dear ones: Caitlin McNally, Noah Waxman, Elizabeth Phelan, Sophia Stamatopoulou-Robbins, Sonya Larson, Amy Krauss, Eva Lucero, Meli Zeiger, Begonya Plaza, Matt Ellis, Erin Yerby, Michael Lukas, Robin Fann and Corey Costanzo, who have discussed the world and writing with me from every angle for as long as I can remember. And to the wonderful Debbi Dunn and Stephen and Sarah Solomon, for being my home in Princeton and interlocutors on this work.

Immense gratitude to my academic advisors, who have helped me, over years and years, to hone the ideas that weave in and out of my poems: Nadia Abu-El Haj, Brink Messick, Marilyn Ivy, and Ronald Nettler. And to my colleagues at Princeton for a rich new home for inquiry: Carolyn Rouse, Lisa Davis, Julia Elyachar, Carol Greenhouse, Lauren Coyle Rosen, Andrew Johnson, Rena Lederman, Serguei Oushakine, João Biehl, John Borneman, and Jeff Himpele. Thank you to my dear cousins Alisha, Eric, Ethan, Gavin, and Jack Benner, who housed and fed and loved me and made me laugh during all those years of fieldwork and beyond.

My greatest thanks to my amazing family: my Rose, parents, siblings, and Eve and Asher. And my Bobie, who helped me enable my great dream of getting an MFA.

And thank you to my many interlocutors in the field who have inspired me: Iraqi and American friends who helped me hone my seeing of this tangled warscape and the costs it has wrought.

ML        4/2019